THE
TRUTH

D1707036

Cover and Interior Design by KUHN Design Group | kuhndesigngroup.com
Edited by Michelle Schacht

Printed in USA

Published by Day by Day Ministries
Estes Park, CO 80517

WWW.DAYBYDAYMINISTRIES.COM

CONTENTS

INTRODUCTION

Hi there.

I know you are going through a hard and difficult time right now, and I am very sorry. When we feel lonely, scared, or not sure of things, that's when Jesus, the Son of God, is the closest. All we have to do is call on Him. HE will never leave us. He hears you and knows everything you're going through. He is there and will comfort you when no one else will.

As you read this, you will notice a lot of sayings that I will use. They are from a book called the Bible.

The Bible is the book God had certain men write that tells us about God and Jesus since the beginning of time. God uses the Bible to talk to us. The Bible is one of the ways God and Jesus tell us how much they love us. The Bible also tells us how to live, act, and think. It gives us strength and courage.

It helps us and encourages us through any problem or situation we have and are going through. It even helps prepare us for future problems. The Bible was inspired by God, Jesus, and the Holy Spirit.

The Bible is the tool God has given us to get to know Him and love Him. Most importantly, the Bible helps us know who Jesus is. He is the Bible, which is also called the Word.

If you are wondering who Jesus is, let me tell you. First, we have to start at the beginning. The beginning of time when the world was made. In John 1:1-3, it says,

> Before the world began, there was the Word. The Word was with God, and the Word was God. He was with God in the beginning. All things were made through him. Nothing was made without him.

CREATION

Look around you. Have you ever wondered who made the world? The mountains, the oceans, the grass, the fish, the animals, stars, planets, and most importantly you and me? God did. He is the creator of our universe. Before God created the Earth there was nothing but darkness.

Genesis 1:1-3 says:

> In the beginning God created the sky and the earth. The earth was empty and had no form. Darkness covered the ocean, and God's Spirit was moving over the water. Then God said, "Let there be light!" And there was light.

By simply speaking it into existence, God made the sky and the seas. He made the moon and the sun. He made day and night. He made land. He made the fish in the sea and the animals on the land. He also made man in Their (Father, Son, and the Holy Spirit) own image. He made man out of the dirt of the earth and breathed life into his nostrils. That first man was named Adam. Then, God took a rib from the man and made a woman for that man. Her name was Eve.

THE TRINITY/GODHEAD

G od is a spirit. John 4:24 says, "God is Spirit, and those who worship Him must worship in spirit and truth." Although you can't see or hear God, He is there. He is everywhere. Proverbs 15:3 explains, "The Lord's eyes see everything that happens. He watches both evil and good people."

God actually comes in three forms: the Father, the Son, and the Holy Spirit. Matthew 28:19 refers to this when it says, "So go and make followers of all people in the world. Baptize them in the name of the Father and the Son and the Holy Spirit."

The Son's name is Jesus Christ. He was there when the world began, as was the Holy Spirit. In John 1:1 it says, "In the beginning was the Word, and the Word was with God, and the Word was God." John 1:14 goes on to say, "The Word, 'Jesus,' became a man and lived among us. We saw his glory—the glory that belongs to the only Son of the Father. The Word was full of grace and truth."

Right now, Jesus is in heaven with God, the Father, and the Holy Spirit. Heaven is a place we will go to after Jesus comes back and we are all resurrected (raised) from the dead and are then judged for the good and bad things we have done. The Bible specifically says, "For we must all stand before Christ to be judged. Each one will receive what he should get—good or bad—for the things he did when he lived in the earthly body" (2 Corinthians 5:10).

Heaven is where we will actually be with Jesus, God, and the Holy Spirit. It is a place where there is no fear, no sorrow, and no pain. There will be nothing but joy and happiness. Heaven is a place where you will live with Jesus. As it says in Revelation 21:4:

> "In Heaven, Jesus will wipe away every tear from
> their eyes. There will be no more death, sadness,
> crying, or pain. All the old ways are gone."

JESUS ON EARTH

Two thousand years ago, God sent Jesus to the Earth to save the people who believe in Him from their sins. First John 2:2 explains: "Jesus is the way our sins are taken away. And he is the way all people can have their sins taken away too."

Therefore, God sent Jesus to Earth as a baby (that's what Christmas is about, Jesus's birth). He grew into a child, a teenager, and then a man. He did everything you do— play with friends, eat, drink, sleep, cry, and laugh. He was sad, happy, and went to school. But the difference was He was and is the Son of God. God sent His Son, Jesus, here because He loved the world so much. He gave His only Son so that whoever believes in Him will have everlasting life. "For God so loved the world, that he gave his only Son, that whoever believes in him should not perish but have eternal life" (John 3:16).

That means if we believe in Jesus, specifically that He is the Son of God who came down to Earth to die for our sins and was raised up from the dead three days later, then we will spend forever with Him in heaven. When we believe in Jesus, we are also to say with our mouths that He is the Son of God. It says this in Romans 10:9-11:

> If you declare with your mouth, "Jesus is Lord,"
> and if you believe in your heart that God raised
> Jesus from death, then you will be saved.

Jesus came here not to judge or punish people but to show love and to heal people from sickness and diseases. John 12:47 makes this clear: "If anyone hears my words and does not obey them, I do not judge him. For I did not come to judge the world, but to save the world."

Jesus performed many miracles, which you may have heard. For example, He healed the blind.

> When Jesus was leaving there, two blind men fol-
> lowed him. They cried out, "Show kindness to us,
> Son of David!" Jesus went inside, and the blind
> men went with him. He asked the men, "Do

you believe that I can make you see again?" They answered, "Yes, Lord." Then Jesus touched their eyes and said, "You believe that I can make you see again. So this will happen." Matthew 9:27-29

He also healed people who couldn't walk so they could walk again. Matthew 15:30 tells how great crowds came to Jesus. They brought their sick with them: the lame, the blind, the crippled, the dumb, and many others. They put them at Jesus's feet, and He healed them.

He even raised people, including kids, from the dead. There is this story in Mark 5:35-43:

> The man said, "Your daughter is dead. There is no need to bother the teacher." But Jesus paid no attention to what the men said. He said to the Jewish ruler, "Don't be afraid; only believe." Jesus let only Peter, James, and John the brother of James go with him to Jairus's house. They came to the house of the synagogue ruler, and Jesus found many people there crying loudly. There was much confusion. Jesus entered the house and said to the people, "Why are you crying and

making so much noise? This child is not dead. She is only asleep." But they only laughed at Jesus. He told all the people to leave. Then he went into the room where the child was. He took the child's father and mother and his three followers into the room with him. Then he took hold of the girl's hand and said to her, "Talitha, koum!" (This means, "Little girl, I tell you to stand up!") The girl stood right up and began walking. (She was 12 years old.) The father and mother and his followers were amazed. Jesus gave the father and mother strict orders not to tell people about this. Then he told them to give the girl some food.

Jesus gives hope to those without hope and to those who have nothing to look forward to. Psalm 147:3 states, "He heals the brokenhearted. He bandages their wounds." Jesus heals those who believe in and follow Him. He shows them forgiveness for their sins. He came for the sick, the poor, the kids with no moms or dads, the widows, and the hopeless.

SIN

D o you know what sin is? Sin is thinking and doing things that Jesus would not be proud of. These include not loving God/Jesus with all your heart, putting people or things above God/Jesus, lying, stealing, cheating, and wanting what your friends have. These are God's laws. First John 3:4 says, "When a person sins, he breaks God's law. Yes, sinning is the same as living against God's laws."

Since we are all human, we all sin, every day. We are not perfect. But if we tell Jesus our sins, He will forgive us. " But if we confess our sins, He will forgive our sins. We can trust God. He does what is right. He will make us clean from all the wrongs we have done" (1 John 1:9). No matter what you've done in your life, Jesus will forgive you. All you have to do is believe and ask. As it says in Matthew 7:7, "Continue to ask, and God will give to you."

CRUCIFIXION

There were some people who didn't like Jesus when He was here on Earth. They didn't like the truth He spoke, so they attacked Him and had Him arrested. They didn't like the fact that all people had to do was believe in Him to get into heaven. After accusing Him of things He didn't do, they placed a crown of thorns on His head and nailed Him to a cross. Jesus died on that cross. He died for my sins, your sins, and even the sins of those who killed Him and had Him killed. He died for everyone's sins. "Jesus died in our place to take away our sins. And Jesus is the 'only' way that all people can have their sins taken away, too" (1 John 2:2).

Jesus, the Son of God, was perfect in every way. He died having never sinned while He was here on Earth, yet He died a sinner's death. First Peter 3:18 says, "Christ himself died for you. And that one death paid for your sins. He was not guilty, but he died for those who are guilty. He did this to bring you all to God. His body was killed, but he was made alive in the spirit."

In this way, Jesus was the ultimate sacrifice.

In the old days of the Bible, a sacrifice was the act of killing an animal as an offering to God. Before Jesus, people had to sacrifice animals so that God would forgive them for their sins. Every time they sinned, they had to sacrifice a new animal. Leviticus 17:11 says, "It is the blood (from the sacrifice) that removes the sins from your life so you will belong to the Lord." But Jesus, being the ultimate sacrifice, has given us the ability not to have to sacrifice animals anymore when we sin. All we have to do is ask Him to forgive us because He has already died and shed His blood for all of our sins. "Jesus Christ did what God wanted him to do. And because of this, we are made holy through the sacrifice of his body. Christ made this sacrifice only once, and for all time" (Hebrews 10:10).

What can wash away our sins, nothing but the precious Blood of Jesus.

Jesus's followers got Jesus down from the cross after He died and placed Him in a tomb. Luke 23:53 tells us: "So Joseph took the (Jesus's) body down from the cross and wrapped it in cloth. Then he put Jesus's body in a tomb that was cut in a wall of rock. This tomb had never been used before."

THE RESURRECTION

Three days later, Jesus rose from the dead. As the Bible says in Matthew 28:5-6, "The angel said to the women, 'Don't be afraid. I know that you are looking for Jesus, the one who was killed on the cross. But he is not here. He has risen from death as he said he would. Come and see the place where his body was.'" First Corinthians 15:4 also states, "That he was buried and was raised to life on the third day as the Scriptures say."

Jesus defeated DEATH and is ALIVE. Romans 4:25 says, "Jesus was given to die for our sins. And he was raised from death to make us right with God." Colossians 2:15 reads: "Jesus defeated the spiritual rulers and powers. With the cross, Jesus won the victory and defeated them. He showed the world that they were powerless."

Jesus spent forty days here on Earth with His followers after He rose from the dead. After those forty days, He went up to heaven on a cloud and is still alive. Before He went up on the cloud, He said He was going to prepare a place for us. Jesus said in John 14:2-3, "There are many rooms in my Father's house. I would not tell you this if it were not true. I am going there to prepare a place for you. After I go and prepare a place for you, I will come back. Then I will take you to be with me so that you may be where I am."

HOLY SPIRIT

When Jesus went back to heaven, He sent the Holy Spirit down to comfort us, to lead us, and to be with us. In John 16:7, Jesus says, "But I tell you the truth. It is better for you that I go away. When I go away I will send the Helper (which is the Holy Spirit) to you. If I do not go away, then the Helper will not come." In verse 13, Jesus says, "But when the Spirit of truth, (the Holy Spirit), comes he will lead you into all truth. He will not speak his own words. He will speak only what he hears (from God and Jesus)and will tell you what is to come."

After you accept Jesus as your Savior, the one who came down to this Earth and died for the sins of the world, then the Holy Spirit will come into your heart and guide you. John 14:26 says, "But the Helper, the Holy Spirit, will teach you every-thing. He will cause you to remember all the things I told you.

This Helper is the Holy Spirit whom the Father will send in my name." Later on in the Bible is the verse "The Spirit of truth will bring glory to me. He will take what I have to say and tell it to you" (John 16:14).

The Holy Spirit is who lets us know we did something wrong. When you feel that bad or guilty feeling because you did something you weren't supposed to, that is the Holy Spirit. When you feel safe and comforted in times when it seems so hopeless, that is the Holy Spirit as well.

THE SALVATION OF JESUS

J esus said in John 11:25, "I am the resurrection and the life. He who believes in me will have life even if he dies." If you believe that Jesus Christ is the Son of God, that He came to die for your sins and was raised from the dead on the third day so that you can spend forever with Him, say this prayer written below. By praying this prayer, your soul will be saved and Jesus will enter your heart and life. You can then take comfort knowing He will be with you all the days of your life and after death.

> Jesus, I believe you are the Son of God and that you came here to die on the cross for my sins and were raised from the dead three days later so I could spend forever with you. Forgive me for

my sins, Jesus. I ask you to come into my heart, come into my life, and be my Savior. Thank you Jesus for this gift. Have your Will be done in my life. Lead me not into temptation and keep me safe from the evil one. Help me to forgive those who have hurt me, just like You have forgiven me. In Jesus's name, I pray, AMEN.

Because you prayed that prayer, and you really meant it, no matter what you do, nothing will separate you from Jesus. We all sin, but when we confess our sins to Him, He will forgive us. "But if we confess our sins, he will forgive our sins. We can trust God. He does what is right. He will make us clean from all the wrongs we have done" (1 John 1:9). After we give our hearts and lives to Jesus, everything in our past has been forgotten, and we are made like new. It states this in 2 Corinthians 5:17: " Therefore, if anyone is in Christ, he is a new creation. The old has passed away; behold, the new has come."

It's important to remember that even though you've asked Jesus into your heart and to be your Savior it doesn't mean you will never sin again. Every person sins. There is not one person, no matter how "good" you think they are, who doesn't sin. According to Romans 3:10: "As the Scriptures say: 'There is no one without sin. None!'" This is also repeated in Ecclesiastes 7:20: "Surely there is not a good man on earth who always does good and never sins."

We cannot get into heaven by our actions or the good things we do. If we could, then Jesus wouldn't have needed to come down to Earth to die for us. This is explained in Ephesians 2:8-9: "I mean that you have been saved by grace because you believe. You did not save yourselves. It was a gift from God. You cannot brag that you are saved by the work you have done." We get into heaven ONLY through Jesus and by believing in Him.

Because we live in a very sinful world with sin all around us, we have to make the decision every day that we are going to live for Jesus. And when we do sin, we must confess it to Him because if we confess our sins, He is faithful and just to forgive us and cleanse us of all unrighteousness.

Make sure not to feel like you have to be perfect because you don't. Remember, it's not what you do or what you don't do that gets you into heaven; it's only by believing and confessing that Jesus Christ is the son of God that allows it.

OUR FRIEND

Jesus is our only hope in a world full of fear, sadness, hate, loneliness, shame, and disappointment. Consider these words from the Bible:

> "I told you these things so that you can have peace in me. In this world you will have trouble. But be brave! I have defeated the world" (John 16:33).

> "God did not give us a spirit of fear, one that makes us afraid. He gave us a spirit of power and love and a sound mind" (2 Timothy 1:7)

When we feel sad, happy, scared, mad, excited—any feeling at all—we need to tell Jesus. He is our Savior and our friend. You can talk to Jesus like you would talk to your closest friend. He listens to each of us and wants us to talk to Him.

It's important that when we talk to Him we thank Him for everything we can think of, such as being alive and having food and water. We can ask Him to get us through any situation we are in, and He will! We are instructed in Philippians 4:6: "Do not worry about anything. But pray and ask God for everything you need. And when you pray, always give thanks."

It is important for us to worship Jesus by telling Him thank you for everything He has done, no matter what we are going through—the good and the bad. We can always find something to be thankful for, even if it is only for the simple things, like waking up, breathing, having water, clothes, and food. "Never stop praying. Give thanks whatever happens. That is what God wants for you in Christ Jesus" (1 Thessalonians. 5:17-18).

Jesus says our Father in heaven cares for and dresses the lilies in the field which are here today and gone tomorrow, so how much more will He care for and provide for you? A lot more! He loves you so much that He sent His only Son to die for you. Read what it says in Luke 12:28: "But if God so clothes the grass, which is alive in the field today, and tomorrow is thrown into the oven, how much more will he clothe you. Don't have so little faith!"

THE EVIL ONE

Once we ask Jesus into our hearts and become saved, we need to be cautious of the devil, who is called a serpent. He is the one who convinced Adam and Eve, the first people God created, to take a bite of the fruit from the Tree of Knowledge of Good and Evil, which God told them specifically not to eat. "God said to Adam and Eve, 'You must not eat fruit from the tree that is in the middle of the garden. You must not even touch it, or you will die'" (Genesis 3:2).

Although they did not die immediately, because Adam and Eve sinned, death then became a part of life. Everyone, from the time Adam and Eve sinned to the time Jesus comes back, will die. Romans 6:23 explains it like this: "The payment for sin is death. But God gives us the free gift of life forever in Christ Jesus our Lord." That means that by believing in Jesus, even though we will all die, afterward we live forever with Him. The Bible says in John 14:6, "Jesus said to him, 'I am the way, the truth, and the life. No one comes to the Father except through Me.'"

So since the devil tricked Eve and Adam to disobey God, we are to be cautious of any distractions the devil might throw our way. This is because the devil is out to kill, steal, and destroy. We can read this in John 10:10: "The devil has come to steal, kill, and destroy. But I, Jesus, have come to give life."

In Colossians 2: 8-10, it also says,

> Watch out for people who try to dazzle you with big words and "smart" double-talk. They want to drag you off into endless arguments that never amount to anything. They spread their ideas through the empty traditions of human beings and the empty superstitions of spirit beings. But that's not the way of Christ. For in Christ dwells all the fullness of the Godhead (Father, Son, and the Holy spirit) body; and you are complete in Christ, who is the head of all principality and power.

However, we are not to be afraid of the devil because, with Jesus in our hearts, he cannot come near us. "We know that anyone who is God's child does not continue to sin. The Son of God keeps him safe, and the Evil One cannot hurt him" (1 John 5:18).

ON THE LAST DAY

Even though Jesus is now in Heaven, He will be coming back the same way He went up after he was resurrected, on a cloud. Resurrected means to come back to life after death. You can read about this in Acts 1:11: "They said, 'Men of Galilee, why are you standing here looking into the sky? You saw Jesus taken away from you into heaven. He will come back in the same way you saw him go.'"

Once Jesus comes back, those who are dead and those who are alive at that time, will be raised up to meet Him in the clouds for the resurrection on the last day. And the great Judgment Day will be here. Again, we can read in the Bible: "Jesus said (to Martha), 'Your brother will rise and live again.' Martha answered, 'I know, Lord, that he will rise and live again in the resurrection on the last day'" (John 11:23-24).

Right before we are all judged on that Day, Jesus will defeat the devil once and for all and cast him into the lake of fire to burn forever, along with everyone else who refused to believe in Him as their Savior. Revelation 20:10 describes this as such: "And Satan, who tricked them, was thrown into the lake of burning 'fire' with the beast and the false prophet. There they will be punished day and night forever and ever."

After we are all resurrected, the good and the bad people will be judged for the things they have done, said, and thought. The Bible specifically says, "For we must all stand before Christ to be judged. Each one will receive what he should get—good or bad—for the things he did when he lived in the earthly body" (2 Corinthians 5:10). The Bible also states, "For God will bring every deed into judgment, with every secret thing, whether good or evil" (Ecclesiastes 12:14).

Those who have refused to pray the prayer I shared earlier and who don't know Jesus as their personal Savior will not have their names written in the Book of Life. This is a book that holds the names of those who believe in Jesus Christ, from the beginning of time until the end of time. This book tells who will go to heaven. This can be seen in Revelation 20: 12-13: "On the last day, I saw the dead, great and small, standing before the throne. And the book of life was opened. There were also other books opened. The dead were judged by what they had done, which was written in the books. The sea gave up the dead who were in it. Death and Hell gave up the dead who were in them. Each person was judged by what he had done."

To the ones whose names are not in the Book of Life, Jesus will say, "I never knew you" (Matthew 7:23) and they will be thrown into the lake of fire to burn for eternity, completely separated from God and Jesus Christ. They will never be given a chance to believe in Jesus Christ again since they did not take the opportunity when they were alive on earth. For those who do accept Jesus as their Savior, He will say, "Come. My Father has given you his blessing. Come and receive the kingdom God has prepared for you since the world was made" (Matthew 25:34). We will spend forever with Jesus in Heaven.

This is the goal of Jesus. John 6:39-40 describes it this way: "I must not lose even one of those that God has given me, but I must raise them up on the last day. This is what the One who sent me wants me to do. Everyone who sees the Son and believes in him has eternal life. I will raise him up on the last day. This is what my Father wants."

Although Jesus died for every person's sins, including yours and mine, it's up to each person to decide whether he or she wants to believe that and accept Jesus as their Savior and have their sins forgiven by Him. We have two choices where we want to spend the rest of our life after we die—heaven or the lake of fire. On Judgment Day, Jesus will separate those who believe in Him on His right and those who don't believe in Him on His left. For those who refuse to believe that Jesus is the Son of God and that He died for all of our sins and was resurrected from the dead on the third day and is still ALIVE, they will spend an eternity burning in the lake of fire. Matthew 25:41 states, "Then he (Jesus) will say to those on his left, 'Depart from me, you cursed, into the eternal fire prepared for the devil and his angels.'" Therefore, it is important for us to take the free gift of eternal life Jesus gave us, by sacrificing His perfect soul for us, and to believe in Him and ask Him to come into our hearts so that we can spend forever with Him after He comes back.

HOPE AND PEACE

Remember the Bible is the gateway to having a relationship with Jesus. The Bible gives us peace and hope. The Bible also tells us everything we need to know and everything we need to do. Second Timothy 3:16 says, "All Scripture in the Bible is inspired by God and is useful for teaching and for showing people what is wrong in their lives. It is useful for correcting faults and teaching how to live right."

Jesus loves you and wants nothing but good for you. "'I say this because I know what I have planned for you,' says the Lord. 'I have good plans for you. I don't plan to hurt you. I plan to give you hope and a good future'" (Jeremiah 29:11). When everyone in your life has let you down, you can have hope and peace in knowing Jesus will never let you down. Trust Him and have faith knowing He is looking after you and wants the best for you.

Jesus says in John 14:27, "Peace I leave with you. My peace I give to you. I do not give it to you as the world does. So don't let your hearts be troubled. Don't be afraid."

Have Faith knowing that Jesus is there when no one else is. Faith is knowing that Jesus, God, and the Holy Spirit are real even though you can't see them. "Faith means being sure of the things we hope for. And faith means knowing that something is real even if we do not see it" (Hebrews 11:1). Look around, look at yourself—God made everything, and without Him, everything would be nothing. He is everywhere.

VERSES TO READ

H ere you will find some verses from the Bible that will help you understand who Jesus is and what He does for us. These verses will give you comfort and peace that only He, through the Word, can provide.

When you start to get upset, sad, depressed, or unhappy, open a Bible or pull out the verses below and read them. Know that Jesus hears your prayers and knows your thoughts. He knew the situation you are in before you were even born. God said it like this in Jeremiah 1:5:

> "Before I made you in your mother's belly, I knew you. Before you were born, I set you apart for you a special work...."

Remember, Jesus loves you. He died and gave Himself for you. He wants nothing more than to have a relationship with you and for you to love Him in return. No matter how help-less you may feel right now, don't give up. Jesus can take any situation that the devil tries to use to destroy you and turn it around for His Good.

Matthew 6:9-13

So when you pray, you should pray like this:
'Our Father in heaven,
we pray that your name will always be kept holy.
We pray that your kingdom will come.
We pray that what you want will be done,
 here on earth as it is in heaven.
Give us the food we need for each day.
Forgive the sins we have done,
just as we have forgiven those who did wrong to us.
And do not cause us to be tested;
but save us from the Evil One.'
[The kingdom, the power, and the glory are
    yours forever. Amen.]

Isaiah 41:10

"So don't worry, because I am with you. Don't be afraid, because I am your God. I will make you strong and will help you. I will support you with my right hand that saves you."

Isaiah 41:13

"For I am the Lord your God, who takes hold of your
right hand and says to you, Do not fear; I will help you."

John 14:6

"Jesus answered, 'I am the way and the truth and the
life. No one comes to the Father except through me.'"

John 3:16

"For God loved the world so much that he gave his only
Son. God gave his Son so that whoever believes in him
may not be lost, but have eternal life."

John 3:17

"God did not send his Son into the world to judge the
world guilty, but to save the world through him."

Hebrews 13:8

"Jesus Christ is the same yesterday, today, and forever."

1 John 1:9

"If we confess our sins, He is faithful and just to forgive
us our sins and to cleanse us from all unrighteousness."

Matthew 7:7

"Continue to ask, and God will give to you. Continue to search, and you will find. Continue to knock, and the door will open for you."

Ephesians 2:8

"For by grace you have been saved through faith, and that not of yourselves; it is the gift of God."

Matthew 19:26

"But Jesus looked at them and said to them, 'With men this is impossible, but with God all things are possible.'"

Jeremiah 29:11

"For I know the thoughts that I think toward you, says the Lord, thoughts of peace and not of evil, to give you a future and a hope."

Psalm 107:1

"Oh, give thanks to the Lord, for He is good! For His mercy endures forever."

1 Thessalonians 5:16-18

"Rejoice always, pray without ceasing, in everything give thanks; for this is the will of God in Christ Jesus for you."

Romans 8:28

"And we know that all things work together for good to those who love God, to those who are called according to His purpose."

Philippians 4:16

"Finally, brothers and sisters, whatever is true, whatever is noble, whatever is right, whatever is pure, whatever is lovely, whatever is admirable—if anything is excellent or praiseworthy—think about such things."

2 Timothy 1:7

"For God has not given us a spirit of fear, but of power and of love and of a sound mind."

Deuteronomy 31:8

"The Lord himself will go before you. He will be with you. He will not leave you or forget you. Don't be afraid. Don't worry."

1 Peter 5:7

"Give all your worries to him, because he cares for you."

Hebrews 13:6

"I will not be afraid because the Lord is my helper. People can't do anything to me."

Joshua 1:9

"Remember that I commanded you to be strong and brave. So don't be afraid. The Lord your God will be with you everywhere you go."

Psalm 55:22

"Give your worries to the Lord. He will take care of you. He will never let good people down."

Philippians 4:6-7

"Do not worry about anything. But pray and ask God for everything you need. And when you pray, always give thanks. And God's peace will keep your hearts and minds in Christ Jesus. The peace that God gives is so great that we cannot understand it."

Hebrews 4:12

"For the word of God is alive and powerful. It is sharper than the sharpest two-edged sword, cutting between soul and spirit, between joint and marrow. It exposes our innermost thoughts and desires."

BIBLES QUOTED FROM
ICB, ESV, NLT, NIV, NKJV

ABOUT THE AUTHOR

Day by Day Ministries was founded in 2021 with a mission to be the Hands and Feet of Christ. Most of us have been at a point in our life where we have to take it minute by minute, hour by hour, day by day. Our problems and needs can become suffocating and overwhelming. However, we can take comfort in knowing that Jesus Christ knows our needs and struggles. Jesus says, in His Word, that we are to help the poor, the fatherless, and the widows. Our focus here at Day by Day Ministries is to help those in need while spreading the Gospel of Jesus. We are here to help provide the simple necessities of life that so many of us take for granted.

If you are in need of help, prayer, or want to donate to this ministry please visit DAYBYDAYMINISTRIES.COM.

Remember, Jesus Loves You.

Made in the USA
Monee, IL
15 May 2023